Greece

by Marc Tyler Nobleman

Content Consultant:
Yiorgos Anagnostu, Assistant Professor
Modern Greek Program
Ohio State University

Reading Consultant:
Dr. Robert Miller, Professor of Special Populations
Minnesota State University, Mankato

Bridgestone Books
an imprint of Capstone Press
Mankato, Minnesota

2004

Bridgestone Books are published by Capstone Press
151 Good Counsel Drive, P.O. Box 669, Mankato, MN 56002
http://www.capstone-press.com

Library of Congress Cataloging-in-Publication Data
Nobleman, Marc Tyler.
    Greece / by Marc Tyler Nobleman.
      v. cm.—(Countries and cultures)
      Contents: Explore Greece—Greece's land, climate, and wildlife—Greece's
history and government—Greece's economy—Greece's people, culture, and
daily life.
    ISBN 0-7368-1547-3
    Includes bibliographical references and index.
    1. Greece—Juvenile literature. [1. Greece.] I. Title. II. Series.
DF717 .N63 2003
949.5—dc21   2002011466

Editorial Credits
Gillia Olson, editor; Karen Risch, product planning editor; Linda Clavel,
interior designer; Heather Kindseth, series designer; Alta Schaffer, photo
researcher

Photo Credits
AKG Images, Berlin, 24, 27, 28; Allsport UK/Getty Images, 50; Capstone
Press/Gary Sundermeyer, 53; Corbis/Bettmann, 23; Corbis/C. Penn, 44;
Corbis/D. G. Houser, 1 (middle); Corbis/G. Mooney, 63; Corbis/Kit Kittle,
18–19; Corbis/M. St. Maur Sheil, 14; Corbis/W. Kaehler, 47; Digital Vision,
cover (right); Imagestate, 10; Kontos Photography, 8; PhotoDisc, Inc., 56; R.
Sowersby/REX Features, 41; Stockhaus Limited, 57 (both); Topham
Picturepoint, 13, 31, 32; TRIP/A. Tovy, 48; TRIP/B. Turner, 20, 35; TRIP/G.
Gunnarsson, 36; TRIP/H. Rogers, 4, cover (left); TRIP/P. Richards, 55

Artistic Effects
Corbis; Earthstar; PhotoDisc, Inc.

1 2 3 4 5 6 08 07 06 05 04 03

Contents

Fast Facts about Greece

Name: Ellinikí Dhimokratía (Hellenic Republic), Ellás (Greece)

Location: southeastern Europe

Bordering countries and waters: Albania, Former Yugoslav Republic of Macedonia (FYROM), Bulgaria, Turkey, Aegean Sea (including the Sea of Crete), Ionian Sea, Mediterranean Sea

National population: 10,623,835

Capital: Athens

Major cities and populations: Athens (772,072); Thessaloníki (383,967); Piraeus (182,671); Pátrai (152,570); Peristérion (137,288)

Explore Greece

The Parthenon is one of Greece's most famous sites. It is a temple that was built to honor Athena, the ancient Greek goddess of wisdom, courage, and crafts. People worshiped Athena at this temple. They often brought gifts in the hope of pleasing the goddess. The city of Athens was named for Athena.

The Parthenon is made from white marble. It was built between 447 and 432 B.C. on a hill overlooking the city of Athens. This hill is called the Acropolis. The Parthenon is 60 feet (18 meters) high, 110 feet (34 meters) wide, and 237 feet (72 meters) long.

People who visit the Parthenon today do not see the same temple people of ancient Greece saw. When new, the Parthenon featured colorful sculptures and a large gold and ivory statue of Athena. These treasures have been removed or destroyed over time.

◄ The Parthenon was built almost 2,500 years ago. It sits on the Acropolis above the city of Athens.

Greece

Greece is the southernmost country on the Balkan Peninsula. It is also the southernmost country of the European mainland. Albania, the Former Yugoslav Republic of Macedonia (FYROM), and Bulgaria lie along Greece's northern border. Turkey lies to the east. The Ionian Sea lies to the west and the Mediterranean Sea is to the south. The Aegean Sea borders Greece on the east.

Greece covers 50,942 square miles (131,940 square kilometers), roughly the size of the U.S. state of Alabama. More than 10 million people live in Greece. In comparison, Alabama has a population of about 4.5 million.

Greece was one of the world's first superpowers. At the height of its power, the Greek empire included Egypt and parts of the Middle East and India. The roots of democracy came from Greece. The people elected representatives to speak for them in government. Today, the country is much smaller, but Greeks remain proud of their culture.

Albania

Former Yugoslav
Republic of
Macedonia

Bulgaria

● Thessaloníki

Thásos Island

Samothrace

Corfu

Greece

*Lemnos
Island*

*Paxí
Island*

*Northern
Sporades*

*Aegean
Sea*

*Lesbos
Island*

Turkey

Leukas Island

*Cephalonia
Island*

*Ithaca
Island*

*Euboea
Island*

*Chios
Island*

*Corinth
Canal*

Peristérion

*Zákinthos
Island*

● Pátrai

✪Athens

*Sámos
Island*

Piraeus

Peloponnesus

Cyclades Islands

Dodecanese Islands

**Mediterranean
Sea**

*Kíthira
Island*

Rhodes

N
W   E
S

Crete

Scale
Miles

0	65	85	105	125

0	25	75	125	175

Kilometers

Geopolitical Map of Greece

KEY

✪ Capital

● City

— Canal

Fast Facts about Greece's Land

Area: 50,942 square miles (131,940 square kilometers)

Latitude/longitude: 39 degrees north latitude, 22 degrees east longitude at Greece's geographic center

Highest elevation: Mount Olympus, 9,570 feet (2,917 meters)

Lowest elevation: Mediterranean Sea, sea level

Chapter 2

Greece's Land, Climate, and Wildlife

Nearly 80 percent of Greece is mountainous. People might expect few types of plant and animal life in a country where much of the land is the same. But Greece's location near the meeting place of three continents—Europe, Asia, and Africa—brings a wide variety of plant and animal life to the country. Greece can be divided into three broad regions—northern Greece, southern Greece, and the islands. These three regions are further divided into nine subregions.

Northern Greece

Northern Greece consists of the subregions of Thrace, Macedonia, and Epirus. Thrace is in northeastearn Greece. The Rhodope Mountains run through Thrace along the Greek-Bulgarian border. A narrow plain runs along the Aegean Sea coast. The Evros River forms part of the border between Greece, Bulgaria, and Turkey.

◄ Macedonia is Greece's most productive agricultural region.

▲ Athens is Greece's capital and largest city.
It is in southern Greece.

Macedonia runs along most of Greece's northern border. The Pindus Mountains come through this area from southern Albania and separate Macedonia from the Epirus subregion. The Pindus run down the center of the country. Greece's longest river, the Aliákmon River, begins in the northern Pindus. Macedonia is known for its fertile valleys. It is the most productive agricultural region in Greece. Thessaloníki in Macedonia is the second largest city in Greece.

The small subregion of Epirus lies between the Pindus Mountains and Greece's northwest coast. The rocky land and poor soil make crop farming difficult, but the area is good for grazing sheep and goats. The region receives the most rainfall in mainland Greece. Snowfall can stay on the ground until spring.

Southern Greece

Southern Greece includes the areas of Thessaly, Peloponnessus, and Central Greece. The Pindus Mountains run from Macedonia through Thessaly and into Central Greece. Greece's tallest peak, Mount Olympus, is located in the Olympus Range on the border of Thessaly and Macedonia. Ancient Greeks believed gods and goddesses lived on Mount Olympus. The rest of Thessaly is a fertile plain.

Central Greece is south of Epirus and Thessaly. Athens, Greece's largest and capital city, is in Central Greece. Large suburbs of Athens, including Piraeus and Peristérion, make the population of the greater Athens area more than 4 million. Central Greece also includes Euboea, the second largest of the Greek islands. Like most areas of the country, Central Greece includes mountains, hills, and small valleys.

The large southern section of mainland Greece is called the Peloponnesus. The 4-mile-long (6-kilometer-long) Corinth Canal cuts across its northern border, separating it from the mainland.

Islands

Greece contains more than 2,000 islands. People live on about 170 of the islands. Greece's coastline— including both mainland and islands—is 8,500 miles (13,679 kilometers) long. The islands are commonly divided into Crete, the Ionian Islands, and the Aegean Islands.

Crete is the largest Greek island. It lies in the Mediterranean Sea, at the entrance to the Aegean Sea. The island contains mountains, hills, and fertile valleys. Crete's largest cities and harbors are located in the narrow plain that runs along the northern coast.

The Corinth Canal is a 4-mile-long (6-kilometer-long) waterway in between Greece's mainland and the Peloponnessus.

▼ Tiny Atokos Island is part of the Ionian Islands group. Many of Greece's islands are rocky with sandy coves.

The Ionian Islands are in the Ionian Sea off the Greek mainland's west coast. The seven main Ionian islands are Corfu, Cephalonia, Zákinthos, Leukas, Ithaca, Paxí, and Kíthera. Kíthera is sometimes not included with the Ionian group because it is so far from the other islands.

The Aegean Islands are in the Aegean Sea between mainland Greece and Turkey. Many of the Aegean Islands formed from volcanic eruptions.

The Aegean islands usually are divided into the northern and southern islands. The northern Aegean Islands include Chios, Lesbos, Sámos, Lemnos, Samothrace, Thásos, and the Northern Sporades. The southern Aegean Islands include the Cyclades and the Dodecanese Islands. About 30 islands make up the Cyclades. Rhodes is the largest of the 12 major Dodecanese Islands.

Climate

Greece's climate is often called Mediterranean. Greece has hot, dry summers and mild, wet winters. On a typical summer day in Greece, the sky is bright and cloudless. Cool sea breezes blow along the coasts.

Most rain falls in autumn and winter. The mountains receive snow in winter. Year-round, precipitation is usually heaviest in the north. The northern Pindus Mountains can get more than 60 inches (152 centimeters) of precipitation a year, while the southern island of Kea can get less than 15 inches (38 centimeters).

Temperatures in Greece are generally above freezing year-round. In Athens in January, the average low temperature is 42 degrees Fahrenheit (6 degrees Celsius). In July, Athens' average high is 90 degrees Fahrenheit (32 degrees Celsius). Along the coast, temperatures average about 40 degrees Fahrenheit (4 degrees Celsius) in winter and at least 75 degrees Fahrenheit (24 degrees Celsius) in summer.

Plant Life

Greece has more than 6,000 species of plants, some of which are native only to Greece. The smell of oregano, basil, thyme, and other wild herbs is common in the Greek countryside. Clearings in both the lowlands and on slopes are often blanketed with colorful wildflowers including irises, violets, tulips, and lilies. Greece has more than 100 varieties of orchids.

Greece's largest forests are in the north. Elsewhere in the country, most trees grow along rivers. Oaks,

Rhodope Mountains

Thrace

Macedonia

Aliákmon River

Evros River

Epirus

Pindus Mountains

Mount Olympus

Thessaly

Ionian Sea

Aegean Sea

Central Greece

Peloponnesus

N
W E
S

Mediterranean Sea

Sea of Crete

Scale
Miles
0   65   85   105   125

0   25   75   125   175
Kilometers

Greece's Land Regions and Topography

KEY

Northern Greece

Southern Greece

Islands

Mountain Range

Mountain

River

chestnuts, and poplars grow at low altitudes. At higher altitudes, firs and other evergreens grow. Black-pine forests grow on Mount Olympus.

Nearly half of central and southern Greece is covered with small shrubs, especially maquis. Maquis can include oleander, evergreen, olive, and juniper shrubs.

Animals

Greece has many mammal species. Wildcats, brown bears, and deer roam Greece's northern forests. Wolves, wild boars, and lynxes are rare, but some live in northern Greece. Jackals and porcupines live in the south. Wild goats make their homes in the mountains.

Greece is home to a wide variety of birds. Pelicans, storks, and herons fly Greece's southern skies. Eagles and falcons nest in the mountains of the north. Migrating birds from colder climates come to Greece for the winter.

At least 200 species of marine animals live in the seas surrounding Greece. Dolphins, swordfish, and octopuses swim in the Mediterranean Sea. Lobsters, oysters, and shrimps live near the coast.

The loggerhead sea turtle is a threatened animal species. The last large colony of sea turtles in Europe lives in the waters surrounding Greece's Ionian Islands. Adults usually weigh about 250 pounds (113 kilograms) and are about 3 feet (.9 meter) long, but they can grow much larger. They mostly eat clams, crabs, and other shellfish. Their powerful jaw muscles help them crush shells.

Loggerheads and other sea turtles return to the beaches where they were born to lay their eggs. As tourism grows, turtles have to compete with people for space on these beaches.

▲ Loggerhead sea turtles have unusually large heads in proportion to their body size.

Fast Facts about Greece's History

Start of Greek civilization: 3000 B.C. (the Minoans)
Year of independence: 1829 (from Ottoman Empire)
Current constitution enacted: June 11, 1975
National holiday: Independence Day, March 25
Current type of government: parliamentary republic
Head of state: president
Head of government: prime minister

Chapter 3

Greece's History and Government

From 3000 to 1100 B.C., two cultures lived on the land that would become Greece. The Minoan people lived on the island of Crete from 3000 to 1200 B.C. The Mycenaean people lived on the mainland from 1600 to 1100 B.C. Through sea trade, both civilizations became wealthy and built great palaces. The Mycenaeans eventually took over the Minoans.

Ancient Greece

The period known as ancient Greece began after the end of the Minoan and the Mycenaean civilizations. From 1100 to 800 B.C., Greece went through what is known as the Dark Age. There was a lack of learning and art during this time. People lived in isolated villages rather than large cities. Few people went to school. The Mycenaean writing system was lost.

◀ People of the Minoan civilization created this wall painting.

Small, independent communities called city-states started to grow during the late Dark Age. City-states were made up of a city and nearby villages and farmland. Some city-states developed a democratic government where people elected lawmakers.

Athens and Sparta were the two largest city-states. Athenians prized education and sport, while Spartans prized obedience and military skill. The two city-states had a rivalry that eventually led to war.

Classical Greece

The period of classical Greece began in the 700s B.C. Greeks began to settle new areas. They established colonies as far away as Egypt. These colonies served as trading posts, adding to Greece's territory and wealth.

In 490 and 479 B.C., the Greek city-states joined together to fight invasions by the Persians, another great empire of the time. The city-states did not stay united. The differences between Athens and Sparta remained strong. Each made alliances with other city-states.

▼ The Greeks and Persians fought the Battle of Salamis during the Persian Wars. This painting is based on an engraving from 480 B.C.

23

Golden Age and Peloponnesian War

Soon after the Persian Wars, the Greeks made great strides in art, philosophy, science, and politics. This period, known as the golden age, lasted from 477 to 431 B.C. Many Greek ideas from the golden age influenced future societies.

The differences between Athens and Sparta led to the Peloponnesian War in 431 B.C. They fought many battles until 404 B.C., when Athens was defeated. Sparta ruled Greece until 371 B.C. Fighting between other city-states increased during Sparta's rule. Thebes, another city-state, took over Greece in 371 B.C. Political struggles and fights between rich and poor people led to the weakening of the Greek city-states.

Alexander the Great

In 338 B.C., the king of Macedonia, Philip II, conquered the Greek city-states. Macedonia was north of Greece. After his death in 336 B.C., his son Alexander became king. Alexander became a skilled and respected military leader.

By 326 B.C., Alexander conquered the Persian Empire. After his victories, his empire stretched from Egypt to India. Greek language and culture spread throughout this empire. Alexander became known as Alexander the Great. When he died in 323 B.C., his generals divided his empire. The generals fought one another for land and power.

The lack of a strong leader allowed the Romans to conquer Greece in 146 B.C. Greek culture greatly influenced the Roman Empire.

Christianity and the Byzantine Empire

During the early years of the Roman Empire, Christianity developed. This religion is based on the teachings of Jesus Christ. The Roman Empire treated early Christians cruelly and unfairly. Romans blamed them for troubles since Christians did not worship the traditional Roman gods. Romans thought their gods became angry at this lack of worship and punished everyone.

In A.D. 313, Roman Emperor Constantine became a Christian. He stopped the mistreatment of Christians. In A.D. 395, the Roman Empire was divided. Greece became part of the East Roman Empire, or the Byzantine Empire. Christianity became the main religion of the Byzantine Empire. This empire lasted more than 1,000 years.

Ottoman Rule

In 1453, Muslim Turks of the Ottoman Empire took over the Byzantine capital of Constantinople, marking the end of the Byzantine Empire. Greece became a part of the Ottoman Empire. It remained part of the Ottoman Empire for more than 350 years.

Although the Greeks lost territory and influence, they held on to their Greek traditions. Most Greeks continued to practice Orthodox Christianity, a branch of the Christian religion.

▼ The Ottoman Turks conquered Constantinople in 1453.

Independence

By the 1800s, the Greeks were ready to free themselves from Ottoman rule. The Greek War of Independence began on March 25, 1821. The Greeks and the Turks fought for six years, but neither side could win. By 1827, Britain, France, and Russia had joined the Greeks, and Egypt supported the Turks. Greece and its allies won. The 1829 Treaty of Adrianople ended the war.

Greece's allies recognized Greece as an independent state. In 1832, Great Britain, France, and Russia made a treaty with Greece that named Otto as Greece's first king. This 17-year-old king was from Bavaria, in present-day Germany.

Most Greeks did not like how Otto ran the country. In 1844, Greeks led a successful revolt against Otto. Otto remained head of state as king, but he shared power with elected lawmakers of the legislature. Otto continued to abuse some of the powers he had through the new constitution. He was driven from power in 1862. The next king, George I, introduced a new constitution that gave more power to the legislature and less to the king.

The Great Idea and World War I

After the borders of the Greek state were set in 1832, Greeks held less than half the land of present-day Greece. Some Greeks lived in regions still ruled by the Ottoman Empire. Greeks wanted to free all Ottoman territory where Greeks lived. They called this plan the Great Idea, or Megali Idea.

Other countries besides the Ottoman Empire returned areas to Greece. In 1864, Great Britain gave the Ionian Islands back to Greece. Greece got parts of Thessaly and Epirus in 1881. In 1913, Greece gained Macedonia, Crete, parts of Epirus, and many of the Aegean Islands.

In 1917, Greece entered World War I (1914–1918) on the side of the Allies, which included Russia, France, the United Kingdom, and the United States. The Allies defeated the Axis powers of Germany, Austria-Hungary, and the Ottoman Empire. At the end of the war, Greece gained control of Western Thrace from Bulgaria. The Ottoman Empire became the Republic of Turkey. More than 1 million refugees moved to Greece from the former Ottoman Empire.

National Schism and World War II

After World War I, Greeks were divided on how the country should be run. Many Greeks wanted to bring back a strong monarchy. Others disagreed. This difference of opinion was called the National Schism. Between World War I and World War II (1939–1945), military officers took over the government several times.

World War II began in 1939. In 1940, Greeks resisted an Italian invasion, but Italy and its allies,

▲ German troops occupied Greece during World War II.

Germany and Bulgaria, were able to take control of Greece. German forces remained in Greece until 1944. These years were terrible for Greeks. Germany used Greek resources for the German war effort and caused huge food shortages. More than 100,000 Greeks starved during the winter of 1941-1942. Others were mistreated or killed.

A group of Greek army officers surrounded the parliament building with tanks in 1967. They seized control of Greece's government.

After the end of the World War II occupation in 1944, a civil war broke out between the Greek government and Greeks who supported a Communist government. Communism is a way of organizing a country so the land, houses, and businesses belong to everyone. In this form of government, the goal is to meet the basic needs of all people. With British and

American help, Greece defeated the Communists in 1949. A constitutional monarchy was also restored. During this time, Greece also gained control of the Dodecanese Islands.

Continued Political Problems

A group of army officers seized control of Greece's government in 1967. They took away people's rights, and set up a military dictatorship. People who rebelled against the dictatorship were imprisoned or killed.

In 1974, Greece's dictatorship tried to overthrow the government of Cyprus, an island nation in the Mediterranean Sea. Turkey invaded Cyprus to keep Greece from taking the island. The Greek dictatorship was defeated and was forced from office.

Soon after, Greece held its first democratic election in more than 10 years. Greece became a republic again. The country approved a new constitution in 1975, officially ending the monarchy.

Greece in the European Union

Greece joined the European Community, now called the European Union (EU), in 1981. The EU was formed to build trade and other forms of cooperation among European countries.

In 2002, the citizens of Greece and 11 other European countries in the EU began using a form of money called the euro. In Greece, the former unit of money was the drachma.

Today's Government

Greece has legislative, executive, and judicial branches of government. Parliament, called the Vouli, is the lawmaking, or legislative, body of the government. It is made up of 300 elected officials called deputies. Each deputy serves a four-year term. Greeks 18 years and older are required by law to vote.

Greece's executive branch consists of the president, prime minister, and cabinet. The president is the head of state and has mostly ceremonial powers. Parliament elects the president to a five-year term.

The prime minister is the head of government. The prime minister is elected by the people, then officially appointed by the president. The prime minister is usually the leader of the majority political party in parliament.

The judicial branch of the national government consists of the Supreme Court. It makes final decisions on cases appealed from lower courts. The president

▼ Greece's Parliament building is located in Athens.

appoints Supreme Court judges, who hold their positions for life.

Greece is divided into 51 departments, which are subdivided into 147 smaller districts. The leader of each of the departments is similar to a governor in the United States.

Fast Facts about Greece's Economy

Major natural resources: bauxite, chromite, iron ore, lignite, magnesite, marble, natural gas, petroleum

Major agricultural products: wheat, corn, cotton, fruits and vegetables, livestock, olives, tobacco, wine

Major types of manufactured products: textiles, cement, chemicals, processed foods, transport equipment

Major exports: textiles, food and beverages, petroleum products

Major imports: food, fuels, machinery and transport equipment

Greece's Economy

Since Greece joined the European Union, the country has built a better economy. Still, the Greek economy is weak compared to the economies of most other western European nations. In recent years, increased funding for education and the creation of new technology jobs have helped improve Greece's economy.

Agriculture and Fishing

About 12 percent of Greek workers farm or fish. Poor soil and dry climate make the country unsuitable for widespread agriculture. Only about 30 percent of Greece's land is fertile. Most Greek farms are small. The largest farms are along the coast. Most of these farms have irrigation systems to supply water for crops.

Greece's important crops make money for the country through exports. Wheat and tobacco bring the

◄ Many Greek farmers raise livestock, including goats.

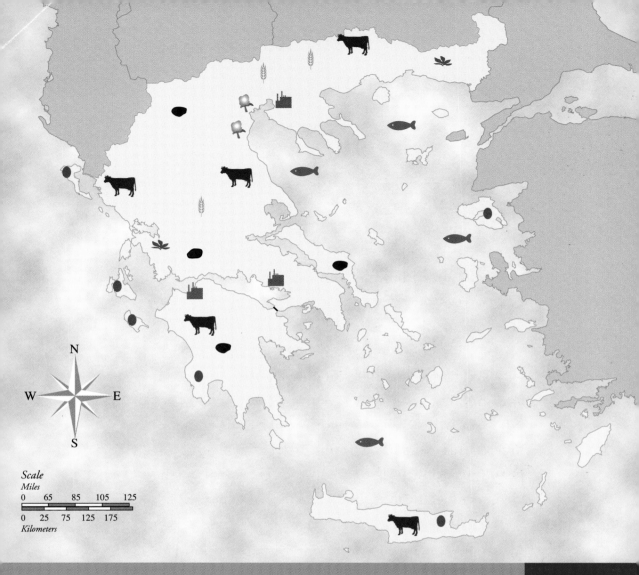

Greece's Industries and Natural Resources

KEY
- bauxite
- cotton
- fish
- lignite
- livestock
- manufacturing
- olives
- tobacco
- wheat

Scale
Miles
0   65   85   105   125

0   25   75   125   175
Kilometers

most money to Greece through export. Greece is a world leader in olive and raisin production. Many of the olives are used to make olive oil. Other important crops are corn, cotton, and sugar beets.

Greek farmers also raise livestock. Poultry is Greece's most important type of livestock. Farmers in Greece also raise sheep, goats, cattle, and pigs. Greece also imports livestock.

Greek fishers catch a wide variety of fish in the Mediterranean Sea, including mackerel, marida, tuna, and sardines. Fishers also catch crabs, shrimps, and other shellfish. Some Greeks in the fishing industry practice fish farming, or aquaculture. They raise fish in tanks or ponds. In the past few years, as many fish were produced through aquaculture as through wild catches.

Manufacturing and Transportation

About 20 percent of Greece's labor force works in manufacturing. Most of Greece's factories are in Athens and Thessaloníki. Greece's leading manufactured products include beverages, textiles, cement, chemicals, clothing, footwear, and processed foods. Greece exports much of its processed foods, bringing in a large amount of money to the country. A newer, fast-growing industry is the production of technology equipment.

Greece uses its huge shipping business to transport its goods to other countries. Because of its geographic location, Greece has a long history of seagoing activity. Today, the country has one of the largest merchant fleets in the world.

Greece's mountainous land makes ground transportation difficult. Most people travel on railroads or paved roads that link major cities and villages. Due to its heavy tourism, Greece has 16 international airports. The largest airports are near Athens and Thessaloníki.

Mining and Energy

Greece has limited mineral deposits. The major mineral is lignite, a low-grade coal. Bauxite, used to make aluminum, is another important mineral in Greece. Stainless steel is made from chromite, another mineral found in Greece. Other minerals mined in Greece include barite, iron ore from pyrite, lead, magnesite, and nickel. The only significant oil deposit is in the Aegean Sea.

▼ Greece's shipping industry relies on its commercial fleet, one of the largest in the world.

Greece uses lignite and other fossil fuels to produce almost 90 percent of the country's electricity. Hydroelectric plants on Greece's few rivers make most of the remaining 10 percent. Greece is exploring other methods of producing electricity, including solar power and wind power. Most households in Greece have electricity.

Service and Tourism

About 58 percent of Greece's workers are employed in the service industry. These industries include education, health care, and banking.

Tourism is a large service industry in Greece. Greece is home to many historic sites and ruins that attract visitors from around the world. Greece is one of the world's top 20 tourist spots. In 2000, more than 12 million tourists came to Greece, more than the country's total population.

Greece's Money

1 euro coin

5 cent coin

2 euro coin

10 cent coin

50 cent coin

10 euro note

1 cent coin

5 euro note

In 2002, Greece and 11 other members of the European Union switched to a new currency called the euro. One euro equals 100 cent. One side of the euro coins features designs shared by all 12 countries. The other side features a design specific to each country.

Exchange rates change every day. In late 2002, about 1.02 euros equaled 1 U.S. dollar, and about .65 euros equaled 1 Canadian dollar.

Fast Facts about Greece's People

Population distribution: urban—66 percent; rural—34 percent

Official language: demotic Greek

Population growth rate: .21 percent

Life expectancy: 79 years; male—76 years; female—81 years

Literacy rate: 95 percent of Greeks older than age 15 can read and write

Chapter 5

Greece's People, Culture, and Daily Life

Greeks have a strong national culture. Their heritage dates back 3,000 years. Today's Greeks use a language similar to the one their ancestors spoke in ancient Greece. In fact, Greek is probably the oldest language in Europe.

Nearly all of the population speaks a modern version of Greek called demotic. This language includes words from other languages such as English, French, Italian, and Turkish. In 1976, demotic became the official language of Greece. Some Greeks also speak English or French.

Religion also unites Greeks. About 98 percent of the people living in Greece are Greek Orthodox Christians. Of the remaining 2 percent, most practice Islam. Most of these are Turkish-speaking Muslims,

◄ Greek Orthodox priests perform a ceremony outdoors. About 98 percent of Greeks are Greek Orthodox.

Greece's largest minority. A small number of people are Roman Catholic, Protestant, Jewish, or other religions.

Urban and Rural Life

About 66 percent of Greeks live in urban areas. About 30 percent of Greeks live in or near Athens, the country's largest city. Most of Greece's cities have old and new sections. Old sections usually contain low buildings, narrow streets, and few sidewalks. The modern sections contain tall apartment buildings, wide streets, and modern shopping centers.

Air pollution is a problem in most Greek cities. Industry and automobiles cause much of the pollution. Air pollution has damaged the ruins in Athens. Greece has taken measures to improve its air quality. The country has banned cars from certain parts of its cities.

About 34 percent of Greeks live in rural areas. The mountains and many of the Aegean Islands are not heavily populated. Greeks in smaller villages have strong connections to their communities.

The population of rural areas has declined since the 1960s. Many rural people are forced to leave their farms to earn more money in cities. Most rural houses have electricity, indoor plumbing, and central heating.

▲ Many Greek cities are very close to the sea.

Education

Education is important to Greeks. By law, Greek children between ages 6 and 15 must attend school. Public education in Greece is free. Children must study the English language from fifth grade through high school. Elementary school ends with sixth grade. The high school program lasts six years.

Learn to Speak Greek

The Greek alphabet has 24 letters. Some letters look like letters in the English alphabet, and some do not. The Greek phrases below are written in the English alphabet. The words look different when spelled in the Greek alphabet.

hello—yassou (yah-SOO)

goodbye—yassou (yah-SOO)

please—parakalo (pa-ra-ka-LO)

thank you—efharisto
  (ef-ha-ree-STO)

Do you speak English?—
  Milate Anglika?
  (mee-LA-teh an-glee-KA)

▲ Greek children pose for a photo outside their school. Schools in Greece teach Greek and English.

Greece has 16 universities and colleges. The largest are the Aristotelion University of Thessaloníki and the University of Athens. Greece also has technical and professional schools.

In Greece, about 15 percent of children continue their education past high school. Many Greeks know the value of a college degree for economic and social success. Competition for admission to Greek universities is high.

Arts

The arts have thrived in Greece since ancient times. People around the world continue to study philosophy and writings of Socrates, Plato, Aristotle, and other ancient Greeks. Greek dramas by ancient playwrights are still performed in theaters. Modern writers include novelist Níkos Kazantzákis, who wrote *Zorba the Greek*. Greek poets George Seferis and Odysseus Elytis have received the Nobel Prize for literature.

Greeks enjoy listening to traditional and modern music. Some Greeks like rembetika, a type of traditional Greek music. People dance to music that features clarinets and a stringed instrument called a bouzouki. Rock and pop music also have a large audience.

Greek artists throughout the country create traditional folk crafts. Weavers and embroiderers make colorful clothes, rugs, and tapestries.

Sports and Pastimes

Greece has a long history of athletic competition. The Olympic Games began in Greece in 776 B.C. Athens held the first modern Olympics in 1896. Today, a different country hosts the Olympics each time.

The Mediterranean climate of Greece is good for outdoor sports. The national sport of Greece is soccer, which Greeks call football. Basketball and water sports are also popular.

Greeks enjoy other pastimes, including travel, watching movies and TV, and attending festivals. Many Greeks visit local cafés to talk with friends.

Food

The Greek diet contains many healthy ingredients. It is sometimes called the Mediterranean diet. Greeks regularly eat salads as part of their meals. Food is commonly cooked in olive oil, which is considered a healthy oil. Lamb is the most popular meat. Greeks also eat beef, chicken, pork, and fish. Vegetables such

◀ Greece (in blue) controls the ball during this soccer match. Soccer is a popular sport in Greece.

as beans, tomatoes, peppers, and eggplant are important parts of the Greek diet.

Spanakopita, a pie filled with spinach and feta cheese, is often eaten as an appetizer. Feta cheese is made from goat's milk. Moussaka, a baked eggplant and meat dish, is a popular main course. Souvlaki is a skewer of grilled meat and vegetables eaten with pita bread.

Coffee, tea, and ouzo are popular drinks in Greece. Ouzo is an alcoholic drink that tastes like black licorice.

Many Greek foods have a Turkish influence, including tzatziki and baklava. Tzatziki is a cucumber and yogurt dip often eaten as an appetizer with vegetables. Baklava is a sweet dessert made from pastry, nuts, and honey.

Holidays and Celebrations

Many important Greek holidays are religious. Easter is the most important religious holiday. At Easter, many families return to their native villages for traditional events. Some communities have candlelight walks and fireworks displays on Easter.

Christian Greeks also celebrate Christmas and Saint Basil's Day. Some Greeks give presents on Saint

Greek Salad

This salad uses many items commonly found in Greece. Balsamic vinaigrette dressing combines vinegar, olive oil, and spices to make this salad very flavorful.

What You Need

Ingredients

2 cups (480 mL) sliced tomatoes

2 ½ cups (600 mL) cucumbers, peeled, quartered

½ cup (120 mL) red pepper, diced

½ cup (120 mL) green pepper, diced

¼ cup (60 mL) sweet red onion, diced

¼ cup (60 mL) black kalamata olives, pitted

¼ cup (60 mL) shredded fresh garden basil leaves

¼ cup (60 mL) balsamic vinaigrette dressing

½ cup (120 mL) crumbled Feta cheese

Equipment

dry-ingredient
    measuring cups

large salad bowl

liquid measuring cup

salad tongs

What You Do

1. Mix the tomatoes, cucumbers, red pepper, green pepper, onion, olives, and basil in a large salad bowl.
2. Coat evenly with balsamic vinaigrette dressing by tossing with salad tongs.
2. Crumble the feta cheese on top and serve. Refrigerate leftovers.

Makes 6 to 8 servings

Basil's Day instead of on Christmas. Saint Basil's Day, on January 1, honors Saint Basil, an early leader in the Christian church.

Greece's Independence Day is on March 25. On October 28, Greeks remember the day their country entered World War II on the side of the Allies. The holiday is named Ochi Day because former Greek Prime Minister Ioannis Metaxas famously said ochi (no) to the 1940 Italian invasion.

Throughout the year, Greeks hold festivals. Major cities have patron saints. Once a year, townspeople celebrate their saint's feast day by attending church, then having a party late into the night. Summer festivals often feature performances of plays or music in Greece's ancient theaters.

▼ Dancers wear traditional dress in a performance for Greece's Independence Day.

▲ This Greek Orthodox church overlooks the sea. The Greek Orthodox religion influenced Greece's national symbols.

Greece's National Symbols

◀ **Greece's Flag**
The Greek flag was adopted in 1822. In the top left corner, the flag has a white cross on a blue square symbolizing the Greek Orthodox religion. The flag has nine horizontal blue and white stripes. The blue stripes represent the sea and sky. The white stripes stand for the purity of the struggle for independence.

◀ **Greece's Coat of Arms**
Greece's coat of arms shows a laurel wreath around a blue shield with a white cross.

Other National Symbols
National anthem: "Imnos eis tin Eleftherian" ("Hymn to Freedom")
Unofficial national flower: bear's breech
Unofficial national tree: laurel

Timeline

776 B.C.
The first recorded Olympic Games take place.

323 B.C.
Alexander the Great dies, ending the period of ancient Greece.

A.D. 395
The Roman Empire is divided; Greece becomes part of the Byzantine Empire.

B.C.   **A.D.**   **500**

1600–1100 B.C.
Mycenaeans live on the Greek mainland.

477-431 B.C.
Greece has its golden age.

146 B.C.
Rome conquers Greece.

1453
The Byzantine Empire ends; Greece becomes part of the Ottoman Empire.

3000–1200 B.C.
Minoans live on Crete.

1821-1829
Greeks wage the War of Independence against the Ottoman Empire.

1917
Greece enters World War I on the side of the Allies.

1944-1949
Greeks fight a civil war.

1981
Greece joins the European Community (now called the European Union, or EU).

1800

2000

1832
European nations recognize Greece as a free country.

1940-1944
Germany occupies Greece during World War II.

1975
Greece becomes a republic with a new constitution.

2002
The Greek drachma is replaced by the euro.

Words to Know

aquaculture (AH-kwah-kuhl-chur)—the raising of fish or shellfish

city-state (SIT-ee-STATE)—a self-governing community including a town and its surrounding territory

communism (KOM-yoo-niz-uhm)—a way of organizing a country so the land, houses, and businesses belong to everyone

Dark Age (DARK AGE)—a time of a lack of learning and a lack of creation of art

demotic (duh-MOH-tic)—a modern form of the Greek language

maquis (mah-KEY)—dense, thorny plant growth that is common throughout Greece

ouzo (OO-zo)—an alcoholic drink that tastes like black licorice

republic (ri-PUHB-lik)—a form of government in which people elect representatives to manage the government

Vouli (VOO-lay)—Greece's parliament

To Learn More

Britton, Tamara L. *Greece.* The Countries. Edina, Minn.: Abdo, 2000.

Chrisp, Peter. *Alexander the Great: The Legend of a Warrior King.* New York: Dorling Kindersley, 2000.

Heinrichs, Ann. *Greece.* Enchantment of the World. Second Series. Danbury, Conn.: Children's Press, 2002.

Kotapish, Dawn. *Daily Life in Ancient and Modern Athens.* Cities through Time. Minneapolis: Runestone Press, 2001.

Macdonald, Fiona. *God and Goddesses in the Daily Life of the Ancient Greeks.* Columbus, Ohio: P. Bedrick Books, 2002.

Middleton, Haydn. *Ancient Greek War and Weapons.* People in the Past. Chicago: Heinemann Library, 2002.

Tames, Richard. *Ancient Greek Children.* People in the Past. Chicago: Heinemann Library, 2003.

Useful Addresses

Embassy of Greece

2221 Massachusetts Avenue, N.W.

Washington, D.C. 20008

Greek Embassy in Ottawa

80 MacLaren Street

Ottawa, Ontario K2P0K6

CANADA

Internet Sites

Do you want to learn more about Greece?
Visit the FACT HOUND at
http://www.facthound.com

FACT HOUND can track down many sites to help you. All the FACT HOUND sites are hand-selected by Capstone Press editors. FACT HOUND will fetch the best, most accurate information to answer your questions.

IT IS EASY! IT IS FUN!
1) Go to *http://www.facthound.com*
2) Type in: 0736815473
3) Click on "FETCH IT" and FACT HOUND will put you on the trail of several helpful links.

You can also search by subject or book title. So, relax and let our pal FACT HOUND do the research for you!

▲ This woman makes macramé bags. Many artisans in Greece embroider and weave all types of crafts.

Index